THE AUTOBIOGRAPHY OF A PHILOSOPHER

G.H. Palmer

THE AUTOBIOGRAPHY
OF A PHILOSOPHER

BY

GEORGE HERBERT PALMER

BOSTON AND NEW YORK
HOUGHTON MIFFLIN COMPANY
The Riverside Press Cambridge
1930

The Riverside Press
CAMBRIDGE · MASSACHUSETTS
PRINTED IN THE U.S.A.

PREFACE

In 1930 the American Philosophy Association dedicated its new volume of discussions to me and asked me to write the introductory paper. I was somewhat puzzled by the honor. It could not be due to any signal contribution on my part to philosophical doctrine, such as has been made by several of my colleagues, by James, Royce, Münsterberg, Santayana, Perry, McDougall. My name is connected with none of the many fighting faiths which have enriched American thought during the eighty-six years of my life. There is no distinctively Palmerian philosophy. But I have viewed the whole marvellous expansion of thought that has gone on from the restricted outlook of Hopkins, Porter, Bowen, and McCosh to the wide horizons of Dewey, Montague, Hocking, and Whitehead.

v

PREFACE

What then is the mental condition of one who has seen it all, seen it, too, instructed by a pretty wide acquaintance with the general history of philosophy? This may well be the question I was asked to answer. Of argumentation over single problems enough was offered by other contributors. They are still in the field of conflict. Something more personal I could supply. By making my paper largely biographic I could treat myself as a kind of representative of the philosophic young men of my time. I could tell of the haphazards, discouragements, helps, and changes of public opinion through which they have forced their way from the stagnation of early thought into the tumultuous activity of the present time, and beyond this into individual careers and positive personal beliefs. Of course each of us is unique. No man is completely typical. Yet there are sufficient resemblances among the buffetings that have fallen on us all to make a single candid story of them interesting and instructive. The plot of the story may fit each, even if the incidents vary. So I have tried to set down here an old man's memories of the struggles through which he has passed in reaching the criticized convictions about ultimate things on which he now relies. In short, through following the instructions given me at starting I have been led into what closely resembles an autobiography.

THE AUTOBIOGRAPHY OF A PHILOSOPHER

THE AUTOBIOGRAPHY OF A PHILOSOPHER

. .

PART I

I

FAIRLY to follow the growth of a mind, one must begin by inspecting the soil wherefrom its roots drew nourishment. From what heritage did I set out? I am of English stock. My father's ancestor came over in 1636 and settled at Little Compton, Rhode Island. A few years later John Peabody, the ancestor of my mother, settled at Boxford, Massachusetts, and on his farm I am of the seventh generation. Half of each year of my youth I lived in the country; the other half in Boston, where on March 19, 1842, I was born. In the same house with me were born my seven brothers and sisters. My father, a business man, was of modest means, so that we early learned the careful use of money. No waste was allowed and we understood that there would be little property to be divided after the death of our parents. But expenditures for education, books, music, travel, charity, and the dignified furnishing of the home were lavish. After attendance at the Boston public schools, all four boys went to Phillips Academy, Andover, two subsequently to Harvard College. Two by their own choice entered business. Self-reliance was secured by my father's principle that every healthy child who had been well brought up should be turned out of the home at twelve. That was my age when I entered Andover. Studious opportunities for girls were scanty then. But from the best there were, each of my sisters took what suited her disposition.

Two strong philosophic influences dominated my childhood, one personal, one institutional. To-day it is fashionable to decry authority in education and allow the child to form his own beliefs. But where shall he get material to form them of? In reality we do not enter the world so poor. Each of us starts with what I may call an intellectual bank-stock, consisting of the conclusions those preceding us have reached in regard to the best modes of living. Knives and forks, three meals a day, electricity, the state, the family, are notions we were not left to invent, but to adopt and criticize.

An uncle of mine, a professor of Latin in Amherst College, had loved the old English poet, George Herbert, and suggested to my mother to give me his name 'so that I might always have a friend.' A rich endowment indeed! For though Herbert's range is limited, he is an exquisite lyric artist who spent the few years of his ardent and hesitating life in perplexity over the counter-attractions of the one and the many, God and the world.

In him religious aspiration is peculiarly fresh and genuine. No less so are the allurements of sex, station, sweet sounds, rich clothes, fine phrases, high society. He always remains a double-minded man, at his death entrusting the manuscript of his poems to his friends as 'a picture of the conflicts of my soul with God.' What a stimulus to reflection would a thoughtful boy find in such a volume!

But the philosophic influence which was supreme over my youth and has left its honored mark on my age was Puritanism. My father was a deacon in an Orthodox church. Four uncles were Orthodox ministers. Religion of that positive type entered into every hour of my happy home. In a former paper I have set forth the facts and features of the Puritan home and shown how far from true are the current caricatures of it. While profoundly serious — more romantically serious than many natures could

well bear — there was nothing morose or
sour about it. If its people had such traits independently, these no doubt appeared peculiarly unlovely in a religious setting. But
for stout and cheerful souls it was an en-
nobling faith, providing abundant room for
the play of all that is worthy in human
character.

According to it man and God are not
separable. A complete man, such as once
appeared, would be a revelation of God Himself. There are, however, lower and higher
sides in our nature, the former expressing
our adaptation to the physical and temporary world we inhabit. These, therefore, require continual subordination to the rational
order. Indeed, the exercise of this subordination — not suppression — is a precious opportunity for that self-discipline which is the
very purpose of our existence. We are born
only half made and must not take any casual
impulse as if it rightly belonged to us. Pick

7

and choose. Life is designed as a training school where each orderly advance makes another more possible. So life here prepares for life hereafter, and in that new life there will be nothing arbitrary. Its woe or happiness is the unobstructed expression of what we have come to value. The Puritan stood face to face with God and owned responsibility to no one else. No church or state could bind him. In his conscience and his Bible — and between the two he felt no divergence — he heard the authentic voice of God.

There are plenty of loose joints in such a creed, especially in its extreme individualism and lack of a community sense. But all will acknowledge that it provides an incomparable body of material for a youthful philosopher to wrestle with. In Germany under the name of Pietism it started the career of Kant. And nobody can understand the early history of America without perceiving that the Puritanism of New England furnishes its backbone.

Such was the rich intellectual 'bank-stock' I set out with. But the physical stock was discouragingly poor. I was born a weakling, not expected to live from year to year. Spinal and heart trouble were in the family on my mother's side; on my father's constipation, rupture, and the attendant disturbances. My whole nervous system was over-sensitive and easily upset. Hardly one of my early years went by without a long illness. There may have been disorder in the brain, for up to about my fortieth year, headaches were almost continuous and I have never slept a night through in my life. I have undergone six surgical operations, the last when I was eighty-three. It is hardly necessary to add that I was a shy boy, avoiding people and finding writing and speaking extremely difficult. I do not complain of these conditions. Most of us break down at some time. He is fortunate to whom ill health comes early and who thus learns betimes how to take care of himself. Since the nervous collapse that sent me home from Germany in 1869, I have been building up a body capable of meeting strains undisturbed. And that is the test of health.

Going to Andover at twelve to prepare for college, I was stopped two years later by granulation of the eyelids. Hard little particles nearly as large as peas formed on the under surface and nearly closed the lids. I was obliged to give up study and be put in charge of a surgical oculist. After six months' treatment he advised an entire change of climate, if possible a sea voyage. On a barque of five hundred tons I at fifteen, with a brother two years older as companion, sailed for Egypt. There we spent a month in a country as yet hardly affected by Western civilization. It was a memorable experience for a youngster, but produced no improvement in the eyes. All thought of education had to be abandoned and I took a place in a wholesale dry-goods store.

After rather more than a year a friend took me to a physician in general practice who thought my trouble might not be merely local, but due to a generally bad condition of the system. With no instruments or lotions, but using simple homœopathic medicine, he brought the lids in the course of a few months to entire smoothness. To let the eyes grow strong they should have had an entire year's rest. But the prospect of entering Harvard was too inviting. I found that by exercising in the open air for most of the day, I could study for an hour or two. As my doctor did not absolutely forbid the plan, I took a tutor and crawled into Harvard in 1860 with six conditions, but with feeble eyesight for the rest of my life. From service in the Civil War I was rejected on account of my eyes.

II

Harvard education reached its lowest point during my college course. When I entered, it was a small local institution with nine hundred and ninety-six students in all its departments and thirty teachers in the College Faculty. C. C. Felton was its President. Nearly all its studies were prescribed, and these were chiefly Greek, Latin, and Mathematics. There was one course in Modern History, one in Philosophy, a half course in Economics. There was no English Literature, but in the Sophomore year three hours a week were required in Anglo-Saxon. A feeble course or two in Modern Languages was allowed to those who wished it. There were two or three courses in Natural Science, taught without laboratory work. All courses were taught from textbooks and by recitations. Though lectures were announced in several subjects, among them English Literature, not more than half a dozen of these were given in a year. Professor Cooke, it is true, lectured to the Sophomores an hour each week on Chemistry. But though we were all required to attend, there was no examination. All teaching was of a low order. The personality of only two teachers impressed me, Torrey in History, Gurney in Latin; perhaps I should add Sophocles in Greek, through his picturesque remoteness.

Such a curriculum — and it was no worse than in other colleges — would seem to have been arranged by a lunatic and to be valuable only as preparing the way for an Eliot. But that would be a mistaken judgment. While students found little to attract them in the official programme, they had four free years to devote to sports, society, discussion, friendships, and the pursuit of individual tastes. There was enormous waste, of course. But any of us who cared for intellectual things enjoyed an elective system of our own. I, up to the limit of my eyesight, read Poetry,

13

Philosophy, and History, committing great quantities of Poetry to memory at times when I could not read. Tennyson was my master. All his changes from edition to edition I copied into a pocket volume and was fairly introduced by him to Poetry as a Fine Art. Art for me became henceforth a close ally of Philosophy and Religion.

What I most wanted from Harvard was systematic training in Philosophy. But Professor Bowen offered only a single course and that more elementary than any of the more than thirty now on the Harvard list. A slender acquaintance with the Scotch School — Reid, Stewart, Hamilton — was something. Something came from a source peculiarly barren, Lewes' 'Biographical History of Philosophy.' It is an ignorant book, written to prove that there is no such thing as Philosophy. But the style is pleasing and the exhibit of an age-long struggle by man to comprehend himself, his world, and his maker, was what I needed at that particular moment. It was my first encounter with historic thought.

In striking contrast with this pretender, a genuine man appeared and made an epoch in my intellectual life, John Stuart Mill. His book 'On Liberty' was published the year before I entered college, his 'Utilitarianism' in my Junior year. Through these I experienced for the first time the luxury of loyalty, of feeling myself a follower and propagandist. In the 'Utilitarianism' I had gained a moral creed and I made my Commencement part a defence of it. Everything that Mill wrote I read eagerly. And though before long I came to see that the best parts of Mill were his inconsistencies, these in no way lessened my admiration. They rather increased it as signs of his candor and freedom from partisanship. Here was a beautiful soul, somewhat too modest and inclined to lean — on his father, on Bentham, on

Mrs. Taylor, on Miss Taylor — and showing in his face the tragedy produced by the conflict between the new idealism of Coleridge and Wordsworth and the traditional empiricism in which he grew up. While Mill's philosophy provided me no resting-place, I have never ceased to think gratefully of the man. On my first visit to England, I went to the House of Commons and found my hero not the calm listener I had imagined, but restless in his seat and continually ejaculating the strange 'Hear, Hear!' with which members approve what is said. In the early nineties Mrs. Palmer and I made a pilgrimage to Avignon to see the house where Mill spent his last years in sight of his wife's grave.

Herbert Spencer never affected me in any such way. His technical knowledge of Philosophy was slight and his personality inferior. Nor was I much moved by the bitter Darwinian controversy. Darwin himself was

admirably restrained, but his defenders and
assailants were alike blunderers when they
assumed that religion was at stake over the
question whether creation was accomplished
at once or by successive stages. On the whole
I thought those wisest who did not count
evolution an affair of chance. These three
men, Mill, Spencer, and Darwin, were the
chief agents in breaking up American stupor
and starting fruitful philosophic discussion.

III

On leaving college I felt I had absorbed
more than I had digested and I resolved to
take a year of comparative leisure for re-
viewing and rethinking what I had read.
Accordingly I accepted a position as sub-
master in the Salem High School. I was to
teach half a dozen elementary subjects with
which I was entirely familiar. But I never
worked harder in my life. To be acquainted
with a subject sufficiently for one's own pur-

17

poses is not the same thing as the mastery needed for impartation. The entire year was devoted to the study of teaching.

Already I had made a beginning in this finest of the Fine Arts. During the winter vacation of my Freshman year I took the place of an absent teacher in the State Reform School. I waked my boys in the morning, presided over their three meals, had them as pupils during the forenoon, for two hours in the evening sat with them in their games, talks, and readings, and put them to bed at nine-thirty. I found them attachable and interesting. Few had known anything like a home or had learned to love anybody. Being somewhat cleverer than the average and more adventurous, they had committed some petty crime and were arrested. Most of them afterwards served in the war. During the later years of my college course I gave two evenings a week to Boston Mission Schools, where all ages, all nationalities, all colors and both sexes gathered to be taught reading, writing, and other beginnings of wisdom.

The boys and girls of Salem were of different stuff. They came of a cultivated inheritance and a preliminary training, and were less afraid of their bashful instructor than he of them. I can feel again the sinking of heart as the closing door shut me into my recitation room with half a dozen pupils from whom I could not escape for an hour. Precious sufferings these. By them a self-centered youth becomes gradually transformed into a public-minded man. Another profitable hardship the school gave; it initiated me into tact. The two Principals, man and woman, were powerful characters, but markedly divergent in temperament. I admired both and learned as much from one as from the other. But they soon declared war and throughout the year were hardly on speaking terms with one another. We all three lived in the same house, sat at the same table, and each required to be treated with considerate care.

These two abilities — the ability to face an intelligent class unabashed and the ability to meet differently constituted people with kindly tact — were begun in me at Salem School. Each was evidently essential for a teacher of Philosophy; yet to make a beginning on them obliged me temporarily to suspend all philosophic work. To devote myself now exclusively to this central interest became my urgent aim.

IV

In most colleges the little Philosophy attempted was usually taught by the President, a minister. If an independent teacher was employed, he also was a minister. Under Puritanism Theology and Philosophy were pretty closely identified. Before the days of Johns Hopkins, too, the best opportunity for continuous study of Philosophy was in a Divinity School. I accordingly entered Andover Seminary in September, 1865. Among the hundred students I met there, I gained some lifelong friends, chief among them W. J. Tucker, afterwards President of Dartmouth, and J. H. Lee, an Amherst graduate who had just returned from the war with tastes similar to mine.

With Lee I formed a studious alliance. We read Philosophy three hours a day, at first in its history, then in the English and Scotch writers, later in Kant. By the end of our second year both he and I felt the need of a broader outlook, especially clearer insight into German Idealism. A glimpse of this we had already gained through the writings of Coleridge and F. D. Maurice. Of course a first reading of Kant had bewildered more than enlightened us. We longed for a German University. One morning Lee returned from a week-end at home with the announcement that his father had told him to spend next year abroad. When this was reported in my home, my brother-in-law offered to send me also. I hesitated, knowing that he was far from rich. But as we all saw that it would be a turning-point in my life and would make me of public value, I finally accepted the great gift, a gift the more generous since none of my family shared my philosophic interests. I hoped, too, that the brain trouble that had been growing more oppressive might be helped by a change of climate.

As neither Lee nor I knew any language but our own, we planned to sail in May, 1867, and spend the intervening months before the universities opened in getting up our German in a family in Stuttgart to whom we had introductions. We would then divide our year between Leipzig and Berlin. The voyage and journey were exhilarating. European travel was less common then than now. To us Europe had always been a fairy tale, and here it was proved real. We ran rapidly over Ireland, England, Holland, and the Rhineland, mostly on foot and in daily wonderment, until we settled in comfortable quarters in picturesque Stuttgart and began our attack on German. As no other language was spoken in the house, our progress was rapid. In July we heard of Tübingen as one of the quaint spots of Germany, hardly changed since the Middle Age, and we walked across the hills to see it. Both of us were completely fascinated. We decided to move there at once and to spend our first semester there.

There for two years I was enrolled as a student, with great profit and enjoyment from the lectures of Professor Sigwart and Professor Herzog and from the intimate personal acquaintance which these gentlemen allowed me. But on the whole my foreign stay was a period of catastrophe and disappointment.

During the summer my brother and sister, who had sent me abroad, crossed the ocean on business and urged me to join them in their Paris apartment. Some happy weeks were spent with them, with the Louvre pictures and with the bookstalls along the Quay. But one Saturday a telegram from Sheffield, England, called me instantly to the deathbed of a friend. It was a stormy night and the Channel boats were crowded. The crossing usually required two or three hours; that night it took nine. I have never known so wild a sea. The waves swept the decks, the hatches broke loose, and everybody was drenched. We landed in the morning with clothes wet through, and before they could be dried, all passengers were called to the waiting train and the long railroad ride. My head was in a bewildered state. I managed to return from England the next day, but as soon as I entered the Paris apartment, I fell on the floor unconscious and for six weeks

thereafter had my wits only at intervals.
The illness was pronounced typhus fever in
the brain. Possibly enough, something of
the sort might have occurred if I had not
been so badly exposed. The brain had long
been weak, the German food was abomina-
ble, hygiene and drainage had there no
existence.

But the upsetting was not without its
compensations. For physician it gave me
Mme. Hahnemann, the second wife of the
discoverer of homœopathy, a stately lady
past seventy, in full vigor of body and mind,
to whom I became warmly attached. Then
as I grew able to move about a little, I
visited the magnificent Exposition of 1867,
where Japan for the first time startled Europe
with its unique art. In the Louvre and
several of the other galleries I studied often,
for Art was now taking its permanent place
in my mind as the supplement and concrete
embodiment of Philosophy. Evenings an

eccentric man of genius, Edward Silsbee, read aloud to me. He was a devotee of Shelley. The Shelley manuscripts at Harvard and Oxford are his gift. I, a sworn Wordsworthian, could give him only a fragment of the admiration he desired. These were therefore gainful weeks. They brought everything except abstract Philosophy. To get this I was anxious to return to Tübingen at the earliest moment. My brother and sister were already in America. Though my doctor advised against haste, I set off as the bleak autumn was changing to winter. It was a bad blunder. I overestimated my strength. A relapse occurred and I was forced back to Paris for another month.

By the time I was settled again in Tübingen, half of my precious year was gone. Lee was to return to America in the Spring and my brain was so unsteady that I was warned not to strain it by severe study. I therefore visited still more frequently the homes of my professors, especially that of Sigwart, absorbing Philosophy instead of studying it. Finally Herzog suggested my beginning a thesis for the Doctorate on the concept of sin in the 'Agamemnon' of Æschylus. At Harvard I had tasted the delights of Greek literature, and little as was my knowledge of Greek grammar I had from time to time read several dramas with a friend. Now in broken health I turned to these enchantments as a refuge. Sometimes alone, sometimes with a like-minded companion, I read Homer through, much of Herodotus, all the surviving plays of Æschylus and Sophocles, half of those of Aristophanes, two or three of Euripides, for whom I never greatly cared. Half a dozen of the lighter dialogues of Plato kept Philosophy alive, but into the magic world of 'The Republic' I did not enter till much later, and I never got much from the 'Laws' and the 'Theætetus.'

It will be seen that my Greek studies were

not serious. A lawless personal taste directed them no less than when I read Goethe, Heine, Keats, or Chaucer, to whom a friend had early introduced me. No doubt such eager amateurism yields something missed by the academic scholar. The two should go together. And in my work for the Ph.D. I more nearly united them.

But I have anticipated and brought over into my first year much belonging to the opening of the second. For there was to be a second. When my father learned of my misfortunes he wrote and offered me another chance. So I spent the Summer in a quiet German village where I could have good care and small expense. By the time the new semester opened, I was much improved in health, able indeed to get real profit from philosophic lectures and from work on my thesis. I need not then recount the experiences of these months, but may skip to the Christmas holidays.

My brother and sister had again come abroad, this time themselves in search of health. They were spending the Winter in Italy and invited me to join them in Rome for the holidays. An interesting time it was to be there, Pius Ninth's Æcumenical Council was in session and Catholic leaders from all over the world filled the streets. Each Sunday I heard Cardinal Manning render Catholicism plausible to the many English Protestants then in Rome. He was an imposing figure and an admirable pleader, as good as Browning's Bishop Blougram. That old Rome ruled by the Pope was worth seeing. The masking for the Carnival was brilliant, the horse-race down the Corso unique, the services at Saint Peter's vulgarly superb, and the Pope's blessing of the crowded Piazza majestic.

But Popes knew nothing of hygiene. The rotten streets of Rome bred a special type of malaria with Roman fever as its product. I was soon attacked. I fled to Florence in time to escape the full force of the fever, but the virus went off in a series of huge boils as prostrating as the fever itself. More than a month passed before I was able to move about and study the frescoes and the lovely Tuscan sculpture. My excellent Italian doctor assured me that I could not expect to be myself again under a year. It was plain that I must abandon Germany, Sigwart, my thesis, and go home. At my little hotel in Florence I had found a dear friend and Harvard classmate, Frank Washburn, whose experiences abroad had been almost as disappointing as mine. He, too, was minded for America. Travelling together slowly, a pair of cripples, we reached Boston in early Spring. Europe had given me little of what I came for, but it had been a great maturing time. A scholar is hardly grown up until he makes another language and another national outlook his own.

I hoped the quiet of a Boxford Summer would put vigor enough into me to allow me a final year at Andover. I entered there in September, 1869. But complete nervous collapse brought me back two months later to Boxford for the Winter. And here let me say that I never became a minister nor applied for license to preach. I saw that my business in life must be the critical analysis of thought, of moral and religious thought, and that any appeals I might wish to make to the emotions and wills of men must be subservient to this and depend for success on the literary power hard work would enable me to attain. In my early youth it would have been accounted presumptuous for a young man to aim at a professorship of Philosophy. He must be 'called' to this. He did not nominate himself. My hope had been to master my subject, preach a few years, and then to be so called. But a change in the educational estimate of Philosophy had been coming about, especially since the appearance of President Eliot. It was not reckoned so audacious as formerly to aim directly at a College position.

Toward Spring an eccentric country doctor began to build me up, without medicine, but with minute instructions on diet and mental conduct. He was a mental healer before medical fashions gave him the right to be. He taught me how to live. The building of a body is a slow business, but I knew myself on the way to it and saw that with study, persistence, and daily self-denial it could be accomplished as certainly as the building of a barn. Now in old age I am in health that may be called perfect — no cold for five years, no headache for nearly twice that time.

V

In May I sent out applications to several Western colleges for a place in Philosophy.

32

None of them replied. One day I met Professor Kelsey, the temporary President of Michigan, Angell's predecessor. As we parted I asked if there were no opening in Philosophy at Michigan. He thought there might be, would look it up and write. While waiting for the letter, I asked Professor Gurney of Harvard if I might use his name as a reference. He readily gave it, but said he thought I made a mistake in treating my subject as final and then looking for a college where it might be taught; better turn the matter round. Choose a first-class college and teach whatever they would accept. If I had power, it would be discovered and I should ultimately be in the place that fitted me. Daring advice! — which I resisted. But three days later, I received from President Eliot an appointment in Greek. I replied that I could not decide at once, but must await an expected letter from the West. 'And how long?' 'A fortnight. If nothing then comes, I shall be obliged to accept Harvard.' Nothing came. Twenty-five years later, President Angell showed me on the Faculty Record my appointment to an Assistant Professorship at Michigan and underneath it, in a different hand, 'Declined.' All were dead who knew the circumstances. The only explanation I can imagine is a letter lost in the mail. The opening of the term was near, a teacher must be secured at once, nothing was heard from me, and my name was crossed off. My entire career was thus changed by a single mishap. So interlocked are luck and purpose in the game of life.

When I told Professor Goodwin that an objection to my entering his department was that I knew no Greek and could not write a Greek sentence if my life depended on it, he was most kind, saying that teachers drilled in Greek grammar were common, but trained in Greek literature rare. One of these would not harm his department. It harmed me, though. Most of my time the first year had to be spent on moods and tenses. In an attempt to make my students perceive what these were for, I offered, as we finished a Book of the Odyssey, to translate the whole at a sitting for all who cared to come. A large number came. Copies of the text were provided and the closest possible rendering was used. Hence arose the voluntary Greek Readings, a plan soon adopted in other departments. In successive years I read the whole Odyssey through twice and in 1884 published a revolutionary version of it.

At the beginning of 1872, Professor Peterson resigned his position of Assistant Professor of Philosophy. I resigned my Tutorship in Greek and was appointed Instructor in Philosophy for a single year on a salary of $1000. This was soon increased by $500, the salary of the Curatorship of the Gray Collection of Engravings, and by the large fees from three private pupils, the last I ever consented to take. Henceforth all my time was to be given to my own subject, in which I was appointed Assistant Professor in 1873, Full Professor in 1880.

VI

But here I must insert a section more frankly autobiographic and sketch in a few words an influence which was the chief formative agency of the first half of my life. Naturally so diffident and self-centered a person had few youthful love affairs. Their place was taken by one abiding loyalty. For ten years I followed Ellen Margaret Wellman, of Brookline. She lived but a few doors from my sister and was an intimate in my sister's household. No doubt I am prejudiced, but I believe every one living in Brookline at that time acknowledged her as preëminent in fascination and accomplishments. A little creature, weighing less than a hundred pounds, all grace, vivacity, and charm, abounding in health and spirits, totally unacquainted with fear either of man or nature, all she did or said was unique, though never queer.

Those were the days when girls did not go to college or take part in public affairs. But the education the best of them gave themselves induced a refinement all their own. Miss Wellman was exquisite in all things, as a musician, actress, dancer, talker. She had read widely and with discerning taste. French was nearly as familiar to her as English. With all her brilliancy, too, and perpetual humor, she was deeply religious, a follower of Swedenborg and the mainstay of her little church. Several years older than I, she allowed me during my Harvard and Andover days all the friendship I could ask — with occasional intimations of a limit beyond which not — until a catastrophe occurred, parting us for a time, but ultimately uniting.

A favorite brother of hers was in the class below me at Harvard. He looked forward to a scholarly life, but was struck down the year after graduation with quick consumption. He was bitterly rebellious. With her usual unselfish ardor she abandoned all other interests to identify herself with him. She must be his only nurse. She did not leave his room by day and slept on the floor beside him at night. When he died he was at peace with himself and God. Up to that time she had never known a day's illness; from that time she knew no day of health, and she never regretted the sacrifice.

The following year she spent in the Azores with little improvement in health but great enjoyment. Her ability to enjoy, no weakness could check. I was abroad all this time. We exchanged a few letters, only a few. But when I came home, broken, too, the love of years could no longer be hidden. It had ripened in us both. Through much opposition from both families on grounds of age, religion, and health, we came to our joyful wedding on June 15, 1871.

The specifically intellectual profits of an ideally happy marriage cannot be summarized. They are too subtle and permeating. But I will venture to name a few of the more conspicuous. Inclusive of all else was the whole-hearted companionship which gave a deeper significance to all I did. She taught me to talk; for we talked all day, seldom of trivialities or gossip, but of things worth talking about. Able to go about but little, she entered the more completely into my work. The publication of my Odyssey was due to her urging, and to her it is dedicated. Innumerable students were drawn by her to our home, and her swift sympathies contributed something to the modern friendly Harvard spirit. Then, too, I felt it an enlargement that the sources from which we instinctively drew our spiritual sustenance were so different. She read her Swedenborg every day and in the early years hoped to see me a convert. But at the last I think she liked me better as I was.

I should add also that the knowledge that we could be together only a short time sanctified those precious years and deepened their influence. For two years after her hemorrhage came, she could only speak in whispers. But this in no wise checked her gaiety or charm. We talked of her approaching death as freely as of any other incident. She advised me, after it should occur, to take rooms in the College buildings, herself selected the rooms, and planned how our furniture should be disposed. On February 10, 1879, she died. For eight and a half years thereafter, till Alice Freeman appeared, I lived among my boys in Stoughton Hall. My life with Alice Freeman has been detailed at such length elsewhere that it requires no recapitulation here.

VII

At the beginning of my teaching in Philosophy, I was merely the Assistant of Professor Bowen. He directed all my work, even what books my classes should use. The Heads of Departments in those days took their positions seriously. Logic was required of all Juniors and I was set to teach it in Jevons' Elementary Lessons. The class was divided into six sections, each of which I was to meet twice a week. Anything less nutritive can hardly be imagined. Jevons has carefully eliminated all Philosophy from his clever and shallow little book, so that my twelve hours a week of work would seem to have been completely unprofitable to me and to my class. But they were not so, and I mention these repellent circumstances because I suspect they are by no means peculiar to me.

Beginnings are apt to be barren. Whatever gains can be extracted from them must generally be collateral, affecting the whole personality. These years proved excellent for the interminable study of teaching. In this I had made a fair start at Salem. But I had not yet gone beyond the bounds contemplated in the common saying, 'I am ready to teach pupils who are ready to learn.' A higher order of teaching should be demanded of a College Professor. He should be able to interest his students in his subject and make them wish to learn. In all my dealings with elementary and required work, this was ever my problem, and I thought myself fortunate to have had it impressed on me so early in my career.

For many years Professor Bowen taught a course in Cartesianism with Bouillier's 'History' as a manual. In 1874 he asked me to offer this as an advanced course, and for elementary work to take the whole Junior Class together instead of in sections. Of course I welcomed this, my first serious encounter with Philosophy. Only I resolved to deal with it in the original, in Descartes' 'Méthode' and 'Principes' and Malebranche's 'Entretiens.' To refresh my knowledge of French, Mrs. Palmer and I spent the summer of 1873 at Saint-Germain. This course I taught for several years with great delight and profit. Descartes has ever since been one of my closest philosophic friends. For the required course a series of wretched books were used, Porter, Bain, Hamilton, etc., the best of them being Ferrier's unfinished 'History of Greek Philosophy.' This enabled me to bring some genuine problems before my boys. When, too, Professor Everett, of the Divinity School, was absent for a year, I had the luxury of teaching Kant's 'Critique' in his place.

It will be seen that at this time all the philosophic teaching at Harvard was historical, the presentation and criticism of notable men of the past. This was the gen-

eral practice of American colleges, whether
cause or effect of the low condition of philosophic thought one cannot say. Probably,
as is usually the case in social phenomena,
it was both. Such habits start in modesty
and the conscious need of knowledge; but if
persisted in to the exclusion of creative work,
they are enfeebling. Learning and origi-
nality are not easily reconciled, essential
though both are. At present too little history is studied. Our young philosophers lack
balance. Fifty years ago they lacked cour-
age. The coming of constructive courses
made an epoch in American Philosophy. I
like to think I was the first to offer one at
Harvard, in 1889. It was announced as
'Phil. 4, A Theory of Ethics Considered
Constructively — Lectures, Theses, and Private Reading.' Into this course I put the
utmost of my powers for twenty-five years.
Because it acquired a certain historic importance through attracting many men who

have since won distinction, I will describe its method in some detail.

No one could take it who had not already spent a year on Philosophy. In its first term every student was obliged to write two elaborate papers, one of them dealing with some eminent writer who approached Ethics from an empiric standpoint, followed by one from an idealist. But in each paper there was to be a sharp division. In a first section the writer was to make the best defence he could of his author's position, regardless of his own views, and not in the author's words; in a second those views were to be stated. The theses of the second half-year were on abstract problems — Freedom, Value, Vice, Punishment, etc., where only the writer's own observations and reasonings were allowed. Meanwhile, I was expounding systematically my own beliefs, interposing at frequent intervals an hour of debate. My system was divided, not altogether wisely, into two parts. The first under the title Goodness discussed the moral individual; the second, on Duty, the claims of society. Throughout I endeavored to impress on my men that until we had rid our minds of all notions of 'radical' and 'conservative' and confined our attention to evidence alone, there was no possibility of useful thinking.

Desiring to avoid large numbers and restrict the class to serious men who were ready to make some sacrifice to enter it, I chose for my hour three-thirty in the afternoon. The course being known too as far from soft, loafers and dullards avoided it and its members were a stimulus to one another and to me. One compliment it received I have always cherished. A committee from one of the tables in Memorial Hall waited on me with complaint of my students who dined there. They made themselves a nuisance. They were forever discussing Ethics and so insistently that nobody had a chance for a word on anything else. That was impolite, I owned. But inwardly I glowed.

And since I have said so much about Phil. 4, I will venture to touch on two points more. While I never wrote a lecture and kept only a continually altered notebook, I found that after going over the same ground for several years I became liable to routine, to reliance on memory rather than fresh thinking. I accordingly learned to drop the course every fourth or fifth year, and when I returned it was re-created. I noticed, however, that it was best the third year after my return, not the first. Royce taught another of these standard constructive courses, Phil. II, Metaphysics. Similar ones were springing up all over the country and were in my judgment factors in breaking up the early philosophic stupor. Notable examples of these were Garman's at Amherst, Howison's in California, Hyde's at Bowdoin. The regular quantum of my teaching after I became

Chairman of the Department was a seminary, once a week for two hours; an advanced
course, three hours; and a half course, elementary, three hours, usually the History
of Greek or Modern Philosophy. Believing
that elementary work requires the greatest
skill in its teacher, we kept it entirely in
charge of Full Professors and assigned our
young men, who were generally specialists,
to advanced work.

VIII

With the Department of Philosophy I
was connected earlier than any of its other
members. I have watched its entire development and have had my share in shaping its
policies. Up to the time of my resignation
in 1913, it included the following Full Professors — I name them in the order of
seniority: Palmer, James, Royce, Münsterberg, Santayana; and for closely affiliated
allies, C. C. Everett in the Philosophy of

Religion, F. G. Peabody in Social Ethics,
E. C. Moore in Christian Morals, and P. H.
Hanus in Education, B. Rand always being
our librarian. It was a remarkable group.
President Tucker of Dartmouth once remarked to me that he thought it not merely
the strongest Department of Philosophy the
country had ever seen, but the strongest
department of any kind. Its powers, too,
were increased by duration, seven of those I
have named being associated together for
more than twenty years. I was in it forty-
one. All, too, had published largely and
made a name in general literature as well as
in their technical subjects. The Professors
appointed since my time have fully maintained the standard there set. As Full Professors there are: R. B. Perry, M. deWulf,
W. E. Hocking, R. C. Cabot, W. McDougall,
A. N. Whitehead. My colleagues were men
of genius who independently would have
had a deep influence anywhere. But I be-

lieve that influence was doubled by certain ethical features in the organization of our department. Since these features have attracted little notice, though in my judgment they are well worth reproducing elsewhere, I name them here.

1. The former controlling Head of the Department was abandoned. A Chairman took his place. This officer called our meetings, presided at them, and was our medium of communication with the President. Every few years he was changed. In the course of time most of our Professors served in this way and so became acquainted with administrative as well as teaching duties. Occasionally even an Assistant Professor was Chairman. But neither he nor any other Professor had authority over the rest. All were equal and independent. When we met for discussion or to draw up our programme of studies for the following year, we did so as a company of gentlemen all alike anxious to

strengthen the Department. If two mentioned the same topic as the subject they proposed for their course on the new programme, we talked it over and considered whether we had better double up, as is sometimes well, or fill a vacancy elsewhere. One of the two Professors always gladly withdrew, postponing his topic to a later year. The Chairman led the discussion and made suggestions, but exercised no control. The fact that no Professor of ours was a subordinate gave dignity to the position and enabled us to call men of superior grade. I never knew any one invited to join our staff who refused. This organization through a Chairman is now, I believe, employed in many Departments at Harvard, but extends itself slowly through other colleges.

2. We avoided 'breeding in' and directly aimed at diversity in our staff. When a new member was proposed, we at once asked whether he had not the same mental attitude

as some one we had already. If so, we did not want him. There is therefore no Harvard 'School' of Philosophy. As soon as our students leave college they are sure to encounter all sorts of beliefs. We wished them to have a chance to study these beliefs under the guidance of an expert believer and then to have the difficulties in them presented by an expert opponent. This, we held, accomplishes best the great aim of a College: it leads a student to think for himself, to acquire the mastery of his mind. It so protects his after-years and saves him from subjection to the casual opinions of his little circle. We endeavored to train leaders, not followers.

3. These differences of opinion in our staff were always openly acknowledged. In our lectures we were accustomed to attack each other by name, James forever exposing the follies of the idealists, particularly of Royce and me, Royce in turn showing how

baseless all empiricism is, lacking a meta-physical ground. One year, James and Royce combined in a course on Metaphysics, Royce occupying the first half year, James the second. One November, Royce asked me to take charge of his advanced course for six weeks while he was lecturing at Aberdeen. I told him I hardly could, for I dissented from everything thus far in his lectures. He said he was aware of this and for that reason had asked me. He thought my coming would 'enrich the course.' I took it and devoted myself to pulling up all the young plants which Royce had carefully set out. When he came home, he ordered a thesis on the entire work of the half year and he told me it was the best thesis he had ever received. Our students were not misled by these our attacks on each other. They knew that we were all warm friends, few Departments more so. But truth was sacred and criticism, the surest way of approaching it, was a friendly, not a hostile process. We wished our students to cultivate the critical habit, learn to be dispassionate, and not allow personal feelings to encroach on intellectual judgments. James has admirably defined Philosophy as the obstinate attempt to think clearly, and nowhere is such obstinacy more needed than for purging one's judgment from personal bias. We were glad to be examples of this, of the honor paid to diversity, and the assurance that infinite reality might be approached from many points of view. And what happiness to work under conditions of entire freedom, where suspicions were unknown, and friendships were profound!

IX

In several of the interpolated years when I suspended my teaching in Phil. 4, I traced the course of English Ethics from Hobbes to Mill. Hobbes was always a favorite of mine.

His eager thought, his frankness, and forth-right utterance made me like to return to him often. I incline to think him our earliest writer of pure prose. His predecessors and contemporaries who wrote something that looks like prose did not think of it as a color-less medium through which thought might shine. They colored it with beauty and meant to have at least half the reader's attention given to the diction, as in poetry. With Hobbes the thought is all. He cannot pause for anything else. The 'Leviathan' is an impassioned cry to his readers to save the nation from impending ruin. The State of Nature is a state of war where each seeks his own, regardless of his neighbor's welfare. The only escape is a social compact where each agrees to give up something of what he desires on condition that others do the same. This is not done out of altruism. There is no such thing. It is merely an enlarged selfishness which by abandoning immediate pleasure reaps through peace a richer harvest.

Here Hobbes set the ethical problem for the next two hundred years. Many solutions were tried. I shall not refer them to their authors. Roughly and briefly as I state them here, it would be unfair to do so. I am not writing history, but merely noting steps in my own progress. Hobbes was told he had libelled nature. It contained two instincts, not one. Sometimes one is uppermost, sometimes the other. Moreover, from our earliest years those about us insisted on our paying attention to their comfort and would not otherwise give us what we wanted. Thus through association the two impulses become blended and we give the more honorable name to the mixture. Or, there is a kind of pleasure in helping the neighbor; another kind in helping one's self. But the former is so much 'higher' than the latter that a little of it outweighs much of the other. Sympathy, the swift experience of what others are experiencing, is too obvious a fact in daily life not to have influenced Ethics. Or, again, Hobbes is right. Our instincts prompt us to pursue only our own pleasure. But in the Bible God bids us seek that of our neighbor also, and threatens us with eternal misery if we do not. It is possible even to ignore questions of *meum* and *tuum* and make morality a simple problem of bulk. 'Aim at producing the greatest happiness of the greatest number' will then be our maxim.

No one of these theories, not even that of Hobbes, fails to honor the claims of society. These are paramount. Apart from society all agree there is no morality. The problem is to find a connection between the claims of society and those of myself. Why should an individual self, a person, go outside himself for an ultimate ground of obligation? Must not life be its own justification? What shall a man give, or take, in exchange for his life? The oftener I returned to this historic movement, the more urgent its central problem appeared. I early saw that self-realization must be our constant moral aim, but only by degrees I detected ambiguity in the phrase.

A child thinks of himself as a single independent being and has never happened to notice that no such being exists. In reality, a single person is a contradiction in terms. The smallest conceivable unit of personality is threefold, father, mother, child. It is true that as we grow the relations of father and mother largely fall away, but this is only because they are superseded by relations more comprehensive. That is, a person is an individual being plus his relations, and these relations are what constitute him to be what he is. What is there in me, I may well ask, that I have not received? What would I be if I were not an American, if I were not a

Harvard man, if I had not had the friends I
have had, or read the books I have read?

Such relations are not external, like those
of space and time. They are constitutive.
Therefore, when I call morality the fullness
of self-realization, the complex character of
the self must be borne in mind. I doubted if
the English writers had felt this ambiguity
of the self and I devised a couple of phrases
to keep the two meanings unmistakable.
These I have since used in my classes and
books with decided advantage. Occasionally and for a special purpose I need to fix
attention on myself in contrast to others.
This I call the 'separate' or 'abstract self.'
The 'real self,' the 'self plus,' I call the 'conjunct self.'

In speaking, however, of the separate self
as abstract and artificial, I do not deny that
each of us is unique, different from all others,
made so by the very relations which produce
the conjunction. Still further, the weighty

facts of praise and blame, and the very existence of morals, testify to some central agency in the conjunct self which enables me to contrast myself as permanent and causal with what happens to me. Rightly I say, 'I have this feeling,' not, 'I am this feeling.' Otherwise it would be as absurd to censure me for a trespass as to censure the wind for blowing. In my book on Freedom I hope I have made this plain. In Royce's philosophy there is something similar to this conjunctive notion. In his early papers when analyzing time he points out how, though we must often speak of a present moment, nothing of the sort really exists, but only a relation to foregoing and oncoming time. And more elaborately in his last book the community is set forth as the fulfillment of the spiritual individual.

I like my term, the 'conjunct self,' better because it holds before the mind with less explanation the nature of morality, the meaning of virtue and vice. Virtue, the service of the conjunct self, calls upon us whenever we act, however slight the action may be, to see that more than our unitary personality is involved. I was walking down one of the paths in the College Yard the other day and saw a man in front of me reading a letter. When he had read it, he tore it up and threw it on the ground. He had done with it; it was of no more use to him. He threw it down, never asking himself whether it was going to be agreeable to other people. That is the very essence of vice. Wherever we trace iniquity it will always be seen to amount to this, the setting-up of the abstract or unitary self against the conjunct.

Something like this seems to have been in the mind of the early etymologists when they coined the word 'obligation.' Translated syllable by syllable, this is 'ob-lig-ation,' 'tied-in-ness,' an excellent expression.

Duty springs from relations beyond the separate self. There is the same suggestion in 'con-science,' which bids us know through connections. When a plate of apples is passed to me and I select the best one, there is nothing wrong in my having a good apple. I am selfish only when I do not consider others and am ready to make my gain out of their loss.

There was one of my predecessors at Harvard who was always careful not to ask a question of his class in Ethics until he had made sure that they could answer it. In those distant days we had only one connection with Boston, an omnibus which ran once an hour. The professor took this to illustrate selfishness. 'Mr. Jones, if you were going to Boston this cold morning and as you walked to the hourly you saw a crowd moving in the same direction, then remembering that the bus had only a single blanket you dashed past and secured

the blanket — what would you call that?'
'Presence of mind,' said the student, a sensible answer for the separate self.

Pleasure is dangerous through its attempt to realize the self in an instant without reference to the rest of life. Evil patriotism tries to isolate itself, to the disparagement of other nations; just patriotism cherishes the characteristics of its own people because they form a distinctive contribution which it can make to internationalism. How disgusting to see a religious sect thinking of itself as the whole thing, instead of trying to be a worthy member of the Universal Church! The jeering soldiery at the foot of the cross laughed at the folly of him who hung on it. 'He saved others. Himself he could not save.' But he was saving that inclusive self of which they were ignorant. Well might Socrates say that the Delphic maxim 'Know thyself' is the starting-point of morality. And I did not discover this starting-point until several years after I had been teaching Ethics! I think this is characteristic of progress in Philosophy. It is seldom an even advance, but on a sudden an obstructing wall goes down and to the prepared eye discloses a broad prospect.

X

It is hard to estimate how great a debt we owe to daily companions, especially to those who differ from us so widely as to set before us a supplementary pattern of humanity. My debt to the men who diversified my Department is simply enormous.

Hardly less is it to the mighty master of us all, so simple, so dignified — President Eliot. He knew little of technical philosophy, but he honored the truth and truth-seekers everywhere. Our growth he watched with steadfast interest and gave us all the assistance we could ask. I was associated with him for thirty-nine of the forty years of his

64

presidency; and living next door to him for half that time, I was privileged with an intimacy which transformed reverence to love. Besides his all-comprehending intellect and his patiently persistent will, I saw his tenderness and the ardor of his domestic affections, and I have felt that he was well described in a couplet of my godfather's, George Herbert,

> He life's way knows
> Whom all his passions follow — *as he goes.*

No personal inclination ever diverted him from an approved end. In consequence of this dispassionate attitude his estimates of men were almost unerring. He liked to surround himself with strong men, and this the more if such associates were critical of his policies. Edward Hooper, Alexander Agassiz, and Major Higginson were choices of his. From him I learned more about the wise guidance of life — and this is philosophy in the concrete — than from any other single man. Perhaps he was the greatest man I ever studied.

I am not sure. For another massive personality shaped me for ten years and in ways more strictly philosophic, Edward Caird. For a long time he was Professor of Philosophy at Glasgow University and probably more influential over Scotch thought than any teacher of his time. Then he became Jowett's successor at Balliol. In those days German Idealism was challenging the Empiricism of Bain and Spencer. When Caird's first book on Kant appeared, Eliot Cabot, the biographer of Emerson, called my attention to it. I saw at once its importance for me and wrote Caird asking to become his pupil for the summer of 1878. He replied that he had taken no pupils for several years, finding his summer necessary for refreshment. I took the next steamer to Glasgow and found him one Saturday morning reading Æschylus in the Greek. He was a man over six feet tall, brawny throughout, shy in manner, and with a strong Scotch accent. After we had talked a couple of hours he said, 'Won't you bring in on Monday afternoon a paper on Hume for discussion?' I did so, and he ordered another on Kant's 'Æsthetic' for Tuesday. Thereafter I spent two hours a day with him, and when he went to Ireland for the remainder of his vacation, he invited me to join him. Some fears I had that all was not going well at home made me decline and return to America. That was the first of six summers, not always continuous, spent with this stimulating friend.

Our procedure was always the same. We took a furnished house and had the owner cook for us, often in the English Lake Country, sometimes in the Highlands where Gaelic was the native language and little English was known. After a simple breakfast we worked in our respective rooms at our respective studies till luncheon time. When that was over, nothing could induce Caird to return to books. We must walk for three hours, accompanied by Mrs. Caird and a shaggy poodle dog known to Glasgow students as the *Ding an sich*. It always rained. I have gone six weeks without seeing the sun. These walks were our seasons of earnest discussion. Returning in time to bathe, to send our wet clothes to the kitchen, and to eat a hearty dinner, we then read aloud till ten o'clock, when Mrs. Caird and I withdrew and left Caird himself for three hours more over books in all languages. A fresh box of them came from Mudie's each week.

He read with extreme rapidity and held at easy command all he had once known. I do not think he had paid much attention to physical science, but in all the varieties of humanism — History, Government, Economics, Ethics, Religion — he was prodi-

68

giously learned. He loved the English poets too, but more still Dante and Goethe. In religion a Presbyterian, in politics an extreme liberal, a propagandist for woman's education and suffrage, he belonged to a club composed half of Professors and half of working-men which met for discussion on alternate weeks at each other's houses.

What I sought him for chiefly was his Hegelianism. He might fairly be called a sectarian Hegelian, for he could find no fault with his master and knew all his innumerable pages. I have gained more from Hegel than from any other philosopher, but I never became an Hegelian. Hegel has too slender a sense of personality and practically none of sin or conscious wrong-doing, a fundamental ethical fact. Freedom is his sacred word, but with him it means natural necessity and has nothing to do with the alternative choice of common speech. My anti-Hegelianism I have developed at length in my book on Freedom. My relations with Caird were like those with James, of friendly and perpetual antagonism.

XI

Two questions were proposed at the beginning of this paper. What agencies have operated in America during the last half-century to transform indifference into the enthusiasm which has recently brought six hundred teachers from all over the globe to do Philosophy honor in the Harvard Yard? Over the answer to this first question I have lingered long in an endeavor to trace the helps and hindrances which attended my slow but probably fairly representative progress. An answer to the second question, about the conclusions reached by an average mind after passing through this transitional period, I have reserved as the topic of the remainder of this paper. Before treating it, however, I had better sum up *in abstracto*

the working agencies of advance which hitherto I have presented only historically.

Table of influences aiding philosophic advance:
1. Resort to Germany for graduate study.
2. Professors make a specialty of single
   subjects.
3. Ph.D. first given at Harvard in 1873 to
   W. E. Byerly.
4. Possibility of aiming at a professorship
   even though not a minister.
5. Philosophic staffs employed in place of
   Presidents or single Professors.
6. For courses beyond elementary, textbooks and mere criticism of authors
   abandoned and orderly constructive
   work expected of Professors.
7. Lectures substituted for recitations,
   with Assistants for quizzes and theses.
8. Books reserved in the Library, and

large private reading demanded of students.

9. Sabbatical years introduced at Harvard in 1878.

10. Descriptive pamphlets issued in 1889 by Harvard Philosophy Department.

PART II

XII

In Religion all Philosophy culminates, or rather, from it all Philosophy flows. To it and to its nearest of kin, Ethics, my life has been given. In the remainder of this paper I shall set forth as simply as possible the beliefs about the two to which the philosophic wanderings hitherto described have conducted me. And in discussing Religion I shall confine myself to Christianity as its universal type. For as we have it to-day it is all-inclusive and readily finds room within itself for the many precious half-truths of the other ethnic faiths.

My ethical beliefs are sufficiently stated in Section IX, page 54. As regards Religion, it will be understood that I am not exploring its rise, like the ethnologist, nor analyzing its relation to branches of Philosophy other

73

than Ethics. I merely wish to show what
place I believe it may rightfully claim in the
practical affairs of to-day. But at the start
a warning is needed against looking in the
wrong direction to find its function. It has
no use as a linkage. When in tracing the
connection of events some necessary step is
unknown, it will not do to call in God to
bridge the chasm. Eventually Science will
discover the absent link and Religion will
be discredited. I have no doubt that God's
agency was needed for this link, but no
more than for every other. The old-
fashioned miracle, where God intervenes to
meet an exigency not anticipated in the
plan of the world, is out of date. I at least
hold that scientific sequence is never broken.

The place where I find God is at the upper
end of the line. Without the presupposition
of God, Science is fragmentary and baseless.
He is the antecedent condition of all being,
the unitary ground of existence. Things of

74

space and time are ever perishing; with them man has never been content. Knowing himself to be in some measure akin to what is beyond these, he has ever been stretching himself up toward an object superior to himself, an object to which he may give himself in uncalculating loyalty. Science needs this transcendent object to impart an 'always' to its truths. A person needs it as an object of loyal devotion. Religion begins, as does love everywhere, with the vision of a person or a cause greater than ourselves to which, approaching with bowed head, we may give ourselves up regardless of personal gain.

XIII

Because Science has been concerned with observation, it has with entire propriety come slowly to the conception of a unitary ground of existence. Primitive races begin with taking each event detachedly and asking no questions. More advanced, they group together similar phenomena and attribute these to the presence of an indwelling god. There is a god of the sky, of the sea, of the winds, of love, of music. This is polytheism and marks a decided advance in rationality. Men are no longer content to see something happen, but feel obliged to connect it plausibly with something else. And this can be best accomplished by thinking of gods of many groups, all separate. A further advance is hinted at by Homer when in half a dozen instances he uses θεός in the sense of a general divine agency.

Now until about a century ago Science had not advanced beyond this point. It talked of heat, light, gravitation, electricity, etc., as separate agencies. But the discovery of the correlation of energies proved that each of these may, under appropriate conditions, be transformed into the others. Whatever happens in one group is affected by the whole. A unitary ground is now recognized with which all things, if fully traced, can be seen to be rationally connected. Therefore, I think we may say that to-day just in proportion as people are rational, no matter what their occupations, they acknowledge something like a god. They do not all call it by that name. Frequently it is called Nature.

But as soon as we are convinced that the one and the many are inseparable, so that wherever we behold a manifold we regularly presuppose a one in the background, two questions await us: Is this uniting one an intelligent being? And if so, what is his moral character?

XIV

To the first of these questions I know only a single plausible answer. For if we must conceive a groundwork of all that is, something in which we live and move and have our being, I do not see how we can leave out

77

of it the element of intelligence. Evolution has gone on throughout the ages culminating in intelligence as its final stage. Can the compendium of all being be destitute of this? Is it not more sensible to think that intelligence has always been involved in existence, but has been only gradually disclosed? Such at least is my belief. Darwinism, attempting to exclude intelligence, is to-day widely discredited.

Furthermore, the view of intelligence as an original factor in the creation of the world seems demonstrated empirically when we find intelligence in nature responding to intelligence in us. The world is adapted to intelligent habitation. While much in it is still blind, the more intelligent we become, the more at home here we are. We are not mistaken in talking about laws of nature. Such paths of intelligent order through what at first sight looked chaotic can even be expressed in mathematical terms without error and so enable us to construct a rational science. Would such construction be possible if we did not postulate reason as latent in all things?

XV

Let me here interpose a few collateral remarks which must be borne in mind as we proceed. It is often said there is no use in going off into philosophical and theological discussion, for such doctrines are always changing. The philosophy of one age is not that of another. When, then, we come upon a department of life that cannot hold its own, why not let it alone? To this I should reply that doctrines of Philosophy do change continually. They never become permanently fixed. I should only have to add that this is far less true of Philosophy and Theology than it is of any other human interest. One might say with truth that the only fixed matter in the world is change. Change is a universal law. Nothing escapes it. In every department of human life it goes on; in every department of non-human life. But there are two kinds of change. There is one sort that sees it was mistaken and sets out again, only to have its new point of view pushed aside by the next that appears. This certainly is a depressing sort of change, but it is not the only kind. There are changes which carry their past with them, which see a deeper meaning than was perceived before and are continually evolving it.

Now when we ask, What are the changes of Religion, Theology, or Philosophy? it must be said that they are predominantly of this second sort. Let any one who doubts that the destructive changes in these departments are less than in others examine any alcove of books on physical science in the Harvard Library. He will find that most of those written fifty years ago are entirely super-seded to-day. They are dead things. What is asserted in them is not true. It is gone. Other doctrines have come up and taken their place. Then if one goes into the alcoves on Theology and Philosophy, he will see that a large part of the speculations and pronouncements of more than two thousand years are vital still.

They are not completely accurate. They stop far too short. There was a depth of meaning in them originally which was not at the time fully discovered. But they can be read to-day with instruction for all. What we are trying to undertake at present is largely a deepening of what is there. They have not been superseded. I would not overstate the contrast, real though it is. Looking back through the ages a scientist will stand out here and there as germinal, opening fruitful paths for his successors. But the history of physical science is of no such consequence in furthering discovery to-day as is the history of Philosophy.

When, then, we consider the nature of an ultimate being, a god or ground of all things, and see that it must include intellect, we must not expect that this will be precisely the same god as was conceived two thousand years ago, or even a hundred years ago. It has been changing all the time because it has been deepening its meaning. I might go farther and say that when any one of us lays hold for himself of that mighty thought, it will appear with a special meaning, different for each of us. No one of us can comprehend in full anything so large. We may look in a certain direction with some assurance that it is a right direction, but our business is chiefly to see how far it can be adopted into our lives, to illuminate and give them strength. That will undoubtedly differ with different persons. We ought not to be shocked at finding that the way in which I approach Religion is different from the way in which my neighbor does. Because each of us is but a fragmentary being, we must content ourselves with fragmentary insights.

XVI

Preliminary education, I have pointed out, supplies us authoritatively with what is generally agreed upon in our community as regards the important facts of life. The University has a different aim. We come to it for purposes of criticism, to gain control of our own minds, to judge how far our inherited bank-stock of beliefs fits our case; what do these mean and mean for me? Nothing is good that has not been criticized, and criticized continually. Some people are afraid of criticism. They say, 'Oh, if you send a boy to college, he will go to doubting everything.' Certainly! That is what he is here for. He cannot come to personal certitude till he has doubted. But I should not agree with the assumption that doubt means simply casting aside. Doubt has a positive office as well. It should bring out into fuller significance ideas which have been hidden under the encrustations of time. And such clarified beliefs are in fact commonly the result. All dictation is taken off during these maturing years. At least we try to take it off at Harvard. Yet it would not be easy to find elsewhere a larger body of serious-minded, yes, reverent, young men.

A peculiarly damaging doubt, however, will early occur to any reflecting mind. Suppose intelligence is inwrought in the framework of things. How vast is that framework! Our world occupies but a pin-head of space in the universe, and in that world I am but one person among incalculable billions. Is it not absurdly presumptuous to imagine that a God of all creation will attend individually to me, hear my prayer, and be pleased or offended at my conduct? Here is a doubt which disturbed the Psalmist and most modest-minded persons ever since. The Psalmist writes, 'When I consider thy heavens, the work of thy fingers, the moon and the stars which thou hast ordained, what is man that thou art mindful of him?'

Now I believe that this inevitable doubt establishes the very opposite of what it at first suggests. To our minds the one and the many are usually set in contrast. In attending to the large we are almost bound to overlook the small. But God, the intelligence of Nature, can have no such limitations. How absurd if He had! Gravitation and electricity are needed for some of the larger suns in the Milky Way. But since there is not enough of these agencies to go round, objects less than an inch in size cannot have them! Is it not more sensible to hold that not a sparrow falls to the ground without our Father? The obvious fact that God is infinite in no wise hinders his being minutely regardful.

Hitherto I have been approaching God on his least personal side, as the intelligence presupposed in the order of Nature. Such an approach proceeds on the principle that with like conditions like results always follow. Without this assurance that Nature presents a fixed order, Science would be impossible. Yet no proof of the principle can be given. It is not a fact directly observed, as for example that sunshine is hot and snow cold. Nor is it demonstrable from anything else. When the sun rose this morning, it brought with it no proof that it would rise again to-morrow. That is a working hypothesis which subsequent experience shows to yield valuable results. When in any case seemingly similar conditions yield an issue different from what was had before, we do not accept the result; we suspect we have misread either the original conditions or the final issue. But in testing the matter we are obliged to employ the very assumption of unproved order once more. In short, this working hypothesis is unescapable. To deny it is to accept it. And this is scientific faith. Not the credulity of the schoolboy: 'Faith is believing what you know isn't so.' Scientific faith, though blind at the start, yields verifiable results.

When we turn to the moral or personal world the situation is much the same. In Section IX I have maintained that the only possible ultimate aim of action is self-realization. There is nothing of greater worth than life to justify living. Only the self to be realized must be the conjunct self. If I set up a separate self and try to realize it, I confront no self at all. To find myself I must go outside myself in loyalty to a personality beyond myself and then through subsequent experience verify that a life more abounding has in fact resulted. Nor will this, if rightly done, be but the experience of a single instance. The moral life proceeds under the working hypothesis of loyalty to a perpetually larger personality. This is religious faith. Religion is allegiance to this unitary basis of all personal being.

XVII

How can we gain fuller acquaintance with God thus involved in our very constitution? By resorting to those who by their superior power show that they have had the deepest experience of Him. This is our method in other departments of human life. Take the recognition of beauty. We have not discovered beauty. It is not anything of my individual creation. It has been in the world a good while and has affected men profoundly. To ascertain its meaning I might turn to Leonardo, who was not only a great producer of beauty, but speculated also on its nature. Shall he tell me what to admire? Yes, and no. I am glad to listen to him, or to any

88

other great master of beauty, and have him point out what it is that he counts beautiful. But I shall not take it on his authority. I shall listen only because I am justified in believing that these men have seen further into beauty than any others I happen to know and I want them to open my dull mind and lead me to see what they have seen. I shall then, casting aside authority, decide whether their teaching accords with my experience and tends toward my strength.

Now precisely this seems to me the way in which I grow in my conception of Religion. I shall turn to those who I believe, and who indeed the world believes, have had the deepest comprehension and experience of Religion and who have united it most closely with life. I should like to come under their tuition and have them explain to me what they have found. Then I shall ask myself whether I can make use of their judgments for strengthening my conjunct life.

89

To-day in our Western civilization we have two chief aids in our comprehension of Religion. They are widely unlike. One of them is a series of pictures describing the experience of a race that is universally recognized as preëminent in its understanding of Religion; that is, we have the Bible. It gives us a series of pictures of a marvellous people and lets us see it grow in its conception of God. It began in the most elementary way where God appeared merely as a tribal deity capable of all sorts of iniquity Himself and approving iniquity in others. Then we can trace that people criticizing such conceptions and mounting ever higher through a thousand years until in some of the Psalms there are examples of the most exalted lyric poetry that exists in any language and all of it impassioned with the experience of God. Here we are taught, by an ascending series of pictures — that is, through history — the meaning of God.

On the other hand, men have busied themselves with consciously reflecting about these matters and have tried to formulate them into the most graphic and rational doctrines. An institution has been erected on this theoretic basis. We have the Church.

To each of us these two authorities appeal. Each tries to point out what we should think about God. Our business is to get as much illumination from both of them as we possibly can and then subject it to personal criticism.

XVIII

Here, then, I am obliged to pass over into an individual confession of faith. I do not altogether commend it to others. They may find modes of approach that fit them better than mine. But when I ask myself where shall I find the deepest insight into the being of God and learn how He can be best connected with my personal life, I have no doubt where it can be had. In Jesus of Nazareth. Confessedly his thoughts about God have shaped all mankind as those of nobody else have. We justly reckon all time with reference to his birth. Even those who maintain that he never lived acknowledge that the legends about him present ideals of incomparable value. Just the same, therefore, as when I sought to learn about beauty I studied the acts and thoughts of Leonardo da Vinci, in precisely the same way I turn to Jesus of Nazareth.

All sorts of stories about him have come down to us. They were carefully gathered, sifted, and reported according to the best understanding of those who knew him. This precious deposit I have and I scrutinize it reverently, but I cannot accept every word that is there. I have to verify it in my own experience, asking would it strengthen me if I, too, thought in that way? I am told that Jesus was hungry as he walked across the plain. He saw a fig tree in the distance and came to it expecting something to eat. Not finding anything, he cursed the fig tree. The story is out of character for him and for me. It is the petulance of a boy over things that work against him, a temper of mind that I try to avoid. But so common is it that something of the sort was sure to drift into the record. Such stories, however, mean nothing to me. I cannot say they are all false, for much that originally I might have called false I now see to be true. Fifty years ago those of us who tried to accept the New Testament had to carry a pretty heavy load when we read how Jesus by a word made sickness cease. These miracles we could not understand. We knew of no such powers in ourselves. It seemed as if such tales had better have been omitted from the narrative. We now see that their absence from the record would have discredited it. To-day it would require credulity to imagine such a being as Jesus moving through the world without such manifestations. We have discovered psychiatric powers in ourselves that were already familiar to him. How much farther their influence may extend we are still uncertain. A miracle is only a physical change prompted by a person.

But more than by unworthy stories, more than by a too easy acceptance of the power of mind over matter, I am disturbed by occasional phrases which may be construed as identifying the nature of Jesus with that of God Himself. This would strike a blow at the work of Jesus in redeeming men. It is true the number of such passages in the Gospels is small and to get such a meaning from them they must be read with extreme literalness. 'I and the Father are one.' 'He that hath seen me hath seen the Father.' 'All that the Father hath are mine.' These are all from the Fourth Gospel. In the three Synoptic Gospels Jesus is sharply distin-

guished from God. God is his Father and
mightier than he. His power is 'given' him.
He is commonly said to be 'sent' by God.
In two passages — and those too in John —
he speaks of himself and God as 'us' and
'we.' His will and God's are contrasted. In
despondency he fears that God has forsaken
him. Several times he prays to God, a
shocking procedure if God and he are iden-
tical. And when a young man addresses him
as 'Good Master,' he rejects the title because
there is only one good, that is God. Duality
is everywhere assumed.

How, then, did Jesus become our Re-
deemer? Paul answers briefly: Jesus broke
down the middle wall of partition between
man and God. Or, again, he was the first-
born among many brethren. The word 'at-
one-ment' would beautifully express the
same idea. But it does not occur in the New
Testament. It is frequent in the Old Testament, signifying a substitutive sacrifice.

But this idea passed away with the Gospel. Each child of God is there called to be united with the Father as Jesus was and to be a vicarious helper of his still alienated brothers. The Synoptists, therefore, and even John himself carefully avoid the outgrown word. Unhappily it was brought back by the early theologians, who found the Old Testament easier to comprehend than the New. Under their influence the King James translators accepted the word 'atonement' in a single passage (Romans V, 11), offering, however, the alternative reading 'reconciliation.' The Oxford revisers employ 'reconciliation' with no alternative.

Recognizing us all as children of God and made in his image, Jesus shows us by his own example that the difference between God and man is only one of degree. There is no such being as 'mere man' nor is Jesus himself mere God. Were he so, he would cease to be an example or ideal for me. A stone bridge may be a model of firmness and of faithfulness in work; but it is no example, for between it and me there is a radical difference of kind. My exemplar must be in some respects my superior, but the more closely he is akin, the more influential he becomes. Jesus undertakes to show us in himself a way of living. Now, if through possessing a nature unlike our own, he is partially immune from our temptations, he would not be for us a genuine way, truth, and life. He would be merely playing a part. I cannot accept so degraded a view. I have experienced too deeply his strength-bringing companionship. Undoubtedly there are mysteries in him which carry him beyond my full understanding. There always are in proportion as one becomes great; that is, approximates God. And how does Jesus approximate Him? Has he made any clear statement of the central principle of his life?

XIX

He certainly has. As I search his sayings, trying to draw from them for myself what made him strong, I find a sacred word to which he returns in almost every utterance. It is the word 'Father.' 'God is my Father' is a summary of his whole teaching. The very words he speaks have no value as his, but only as they are the words of his Father.

Here I seem to lay hold of something which illuminates all life and brings me strength continually. For what is a father's aim? If he is a true father, if he is working out to the full the functions of a father, he endeavors to educate his child, to bring out his powers on every side, to lead him into abundance of life. He does not, if he is a good father, make the child subservient to his own needs. He makes himself subservient to the needs of the child. He adjusts and limits himself so that the child may understand him. He makes it his first business to endear

98

the child to him and himself to the child. He shows how under all circumstances the child may resort to him with assurance of supporting strength. Where there is such a true father, the union of the two is in spirit complete.

Jesus teaches, then, that God can only be thought of rightly as a father. Divine relations he would seem to hold are only human relations, carried to a degree of development impossible here. This Jesus proclaims as a Gospel, good news to the world. Let us consider it a moment and see if it is not truly good news. There is no such thing as blind fate. God is our friend. Everything He allows to happen is intended for our good; not good in itself — whatever that may mean — but always an opportunity which if heartily accepted will yield good for ourselves and others.

It may be objected that this interpretation of divine relations by human is anthropomorphic, and we all remember the denunciation of anthropomorphism extending from Xenophanes in the seventh century before Christ to Matthew Arnold in our own. Xenophanes urged that if horses and oxen were to represent gods they would figure them as horses and oxen. Men are doing the same thing. And why should they not? Certainly a horse-god would fall far short of what we know. But how could a horse come nearer than by seeing something divine in his own power, patience, loyalty, and love? Those parts of him that depend on physical conditions here — legs, lungs, mane, hoofs — he might wisely omit, since he knows nothing about the conditions of life elsewhere. Those found of value in all living things he might more safely trust. In short, what he would need would be discrimination in kind. The Psalmist is soberer. He lets his god say, 'Thou thoughtest that I was *altogether* such an one as thyself.' Jesus frankly treats fatherhood anthropomorphically. This fact sho___ ___ ne in mind when we read the tw___ ___ssages in which the father's act i___ ___ pollution and a long train of disas___ ___ched on the modern world. There ___ ___nce that this attack on the family ___ ___ Virgin Birth was known to Jesu___ ___ to his mother, his disciples, or to ___

The Good Nev___ ___atherhood of God I accept, and find ___ ___ly strength. Two inferior forms of h___ ___ have often appeared. One of them ___ ___ism, the refusal to be crushed, the sen___ ___ inner dignity which enables me to sta___ ___ my own feet, no matter what happens. ___ ___nd of milder aspect is the habit of looking on the bright side. In everything one side is brighter than another. Let me turn my face in that direction. Before Jesus revealed the strength available through the fatherhood of God, these palliatives had value. But they are

superficial and do not touch the sources of
inner peace as do the words of Jesus. Not
that he was the first to utter them. They are
rooted too deeply in reality for that. Ζεύς
Πατήρ, Jupiter, had been heard of for centu-
ries, but like θεός had gone on deepening its
meaning till on the lips of Jesus it became
capacious enough to hold love.

XX

That God was his father was then the
central teaching of Jesus. That tremendous
truth fixedly embodied in his life made him
not only the King of the Jews but of mankind. I want to summarize briefly some of
the varieties of power that came to him
through this understanding. They are open
to us all. In my own small way I have experienced them and know the support they
offer.

Chief among them is companionship. I
am never left alone. Whatever happens

brings me God's kind voice and an opportunity for growth coupled with boun-
teous outgo. This immediate intercourse
with a loved companion is the feature of the
Gospel of Jesus dearest to the mystic in
every age, and justly so. It was constant in
the mind of the Master, turning seemingly
severe experiences into occasions of joy and
blessing. But many mystics overlook the
conjunct self and seek to come into intimacy
with God by removing themselves from
men, going into a cloister, stripping off
fleshly powers, and making themselves as
miserable as possible. They fancy they
commend themselves to their father when
reduced to a minimum. This negative path
turns men away from Him who came to
bring us the abounding life of God.

Fears cease. The only thing worth being
afraid of is now seen to be fear. That is dis-
loyalty. It assumes that our Father has evil
in store for us. But any one who has tried

will find that his constant care can be trusted. Even death prepared by Him becomes a deeply interesting but not appalling adventure. 'Father, into thy hands I commend my spirit.'

Regret, fear of our erroneous past, is banished too. No sin is truly repented until through comprehension and counter-activity we are actually bettered by its occurrence. Sitting in gloom and dwelling on our foulness will not commend us to God.

Faith in fatherhood removes harshness from duty. Love transforms it. It becomes a kind indication of what had better be done to secure the largest ultimate freedom. Or if I fail at once to feel that kindness, I at least know the blessings I have been receiving from my Father; and here is an indication of what He will gladly receive in return; gladly I give it.

A foolish father, still more frequently a foolish mother, lets a child grow up in indulgent ease. A wise father develops his child by frequent hardships. He counts it no unkindness to send his son out on a wintry morning to buy food for the family. To most of us our heavenly Father assigns severities in gaining food, clothing, and shelter. Even if such severities are not in themselves goods ready made, they are—better still—opportunities for developing alertness, resource, and natural continuance of useful work.

Nor are such disciplinary difficulties physical only. We are offered abundant mental perplexities. Our Father might originally have supplied us with all needful scientific knowledge, instead of leaving it for age-long search. And what a petty universe we should have had and what elementary minds!

What takes long in the training of a child and what our heavenly Father is especially careful to train us in is the overcoming of time. Very gradually we acquire patience and learn to prefer a future good to an immediate. Our Father has arranged that the rush for immediate good shall usually defeat itself and in the long run bring injury. He generally suggests the direction we should take. But the most frequent of his prescriptions is to wait.

Perhaps the most important training a father ever gives his child is an understanding of self-sacrifice, so-called; that is, the putting away of the separate self and learning how important the conjunctive elements are, far more so than anything attainable in our isolated capacity. The call to regard mankind as my brothers is only another form of the call to regard God as my father. According to Jesus the two together fulfill all righteousness. How closely he knitted them in his own case! Open-eyed he accepted death that others might have life, and though he felt the pang, he had no wish to escape it. 'For this cause came I into the world.'

XXI

Such acceptance of the guidance of a heavenly Father is neither fatalism nor pessimism. Fatalism lives in a locked-up world where personality has no place. Everything happens because of a central unintentional 'it.' Jesus and his followers change 'it' to 'he,' and so make room for selective action on the part of God and ourselves. Nor is it optimism. It does not assert that all that happens is good. On the contrary, it is steadily contending with Evil and will no longer employ such phrases as 'good events' and 'bad events.' Events become good or bad according as they are used. Our Father furnishes us opportunities only. Out of whatever He sends good can be drawn, but so can evil. Optimism seems to me more immoral than pessimism, for pessimism warns us of danger, while optimism lulls into false security.

But a serious problem remains. How explain a loving God's government of an evil world? There can be no doubt that evil abounds. We encounter it every day, particularly in ourselves. Is then God limited in will or in power? In will, I maintain, and in that fact I find no aspersion on the being of such a God as I have described. Jesus interprets divine relationships by human. Now I have said that a wise father limits himself. He does not take his son and force him to go through certain acts. He does not impose himself on his child. He tries to develop the child's own desires and powers. He assists him, he shows him how he himself lives, he offers him every opportunity. But he expects the child to grow by experience, even experience of error. We might think that an infinite God would be able to stop all evil at once. The heavenly Father of Jesus is too loving for that. Perhaps his limitation of Himself for the sake of his

children will be best understood by watching
the same principle at work in modern education. At Harvard we must confess there are
many loafers, men squandering time and
opportunity and forming habits pretty sure
to unfit them later for grappling successfully
with the world. How shocking to tolerate
such a mass of unintelligent evil! Are the
officials here men of limited ability or do
they care nothing for their charges? Why
do they not put a stop to this waste? The
answer would be that their ability is limited,
self-limited. They know that a student
forced, as the routine education of the past
attempted to force him, is no student at all.
They therefore limit themselves to offering
opportunities, to making those opportunities
attractive, and letting the ultimate guidance, even if erroneous, be in the student's
own hands. Men of independent intelligence
are therefore trained here to-day to a degree
unknown of old. Our Father in Heaven had

been using the elective system long before we discovered it.

Though Jesus announces his Gospel as a universal one, several passages in the New Testament have an exclusive sound. Matthew says that Jesus shall save his people from their sins; John, that the world through Jesus might be saved; and Peter, in the Acts, that there is no other name given among men whereby we must be saved. But it should be noticed that wherever salvation is spoken of, salvation from sin is meant, not merely salvation from its future consequences. Yet even so, what becomes of the numberless tribes of men who never heard of Jesus? If we accept the teaching of Jesus and agree to see in human fatherhood a revelation of God, I think we shall consider the case of the heathen less forlorn than is often assumed. Each family has within it an outline representative of the Most High. Let this be studied and lived up to and Jesus' only way of redemption will be adopted. However superior our advantage is in beholding the great exemplar, no home has been left altogether desolate.

XXII

Such is my religious faith. In the midst of a perplexing world it leaves me peacefully at home in my Father's house, with plenty of work still to do, but with the inspiration of knowing myself a fellow-worker with God and with the multitude of his other children.

And since I have written at such length upon Religion, only a few words need be added on the relation of Religion and Ethics. So far as their contents are concerned, the two do not differ. There is no act which is an essentially religious act. Its religious character depends on how it is approached. When we view it as it would be viewed by our Father in Heaven, it is religious. Athletics is the opportunity for my obtaining a sound physical body and learning the care of my health. It is then as religious an act as going to a prayer meeting. There is, in short, no act which belongs peculiarly to Religion. The Psalmist expresses this unqualifiedly (Ps. XV):

'Lord, who shall abide in thy tabernacle? who shall dwell in thy holy hill?

'He that walketh uprightly, and worketh righteousness, and speaketh the truth in his heart.

'He that backbiteth not with his tongue, nor doeth evil to his neighbour, nor taketh up a reproach against his neighbour.

'In whose eyes a vile person is contemned; but he honoureth them that fear the Lord. He that sweareth to his own hurt, and changeth not.

'He that putteth not out his money to usury, nor taketh reward against the innocent. He that doeth these things shall never be moved.'

Such a sketch of the simplest moral acts is a code of Religion also. Only the mental attitudes differ. In Religion I face my Father; in morals, my fellow man, and each is supplemental to the other.

XXIII

It remains to state my belief about conscience and the objective ground of morals. Have we, as the Quakers say, an oracle within the breast which if we only listen will tell us infallibly in every situation what is the right course? I do not think so. Such extreme individualism disintegrates society and leaves no room to profit by experience. In this matter I am a follower of Jesus and of Kant.

Jesus held that the Ten Commandments were the best code of conduct then known; that we should not let our acts conflict with their precepts nor even with their deeper implications. But he warns his hearers not

to imagine that there are here ten pieces of
righteousness laid side by side, each with an
independent claim. On the contrary, they
are merely varied announcements, predominantly negative, of the fundamental
command to love God and our neighbor, the
seemingly double precept resolving itself on
reflection into a single mental attitude. The
lifelong contention of Jesus with the Pharisees turns on precisely this point. The
Pharisees were not the hypocrites we picture.
They were the holy men of their age, in-
sistent that there is an objective righteousness for each occasion which should be
searched out by the wise and followed
authoritatively by the common folk. This
casuistry Jesus denounces. Let each man
be impassioned with a love of righteousness
and then become instructed about its diverse
workings through his own daily experience.
Jesus did not deny that it is well to wash
before eating or that it is wise to consecrate

certain days to other than secular uses. But
he did object to having these acts standard-
ized, determined once for all by some authority. To be significant they should be
kept fresh and flexible. Undoubtedly the
Pharisees were right in calling the method
of Jesus dangerous. We can only answer
that it is less dangerous to the higher life
than leaning on any authority without or
within. By stopping criticism and individual initiative, Pharisaism prevents
growth and with it that abundance of life
which Jesus came to proclaim. The Catholic
Church, in its sagacious instructions for the
confessional, has followed the moral method
of the Pharisees. Protestants have preferred
the opposite dangers, and they have been
large. Nevertheless, I am a Protestant!

Briefly stated, the doctrine of Kant is that
'ought,' the imperative of duty, is ordinarily
a hypothetical imperative — that is, a command involving conditions. It is, therefore,

of no effect when the condition fails. 'You ought not to smoke. It weakens the heart.' 'But I do not care whether my heart is weak or strong.' Then for you there is no command. Such are imperatives in general. They turn on some covert hypothesis, which is not present in every case. Is there, however, any unconditional, objective, or Categorical Imperative which underlies all others and is unaffected by circumstances? There is, but there is only one. It may be stated thus: Act as if the maxim of your action were to become by your will a universal law. There are other formulations of this, but all amount to the same thing, namely, the only universal duty is the duty of respecting duty. Royce, holding that loyalty comes nearest to a complete expression of moral obligation, was asked, 'Loyalty to what?' and answered, 'Loyalty to loyalty.' That was his Categorical Imperative, the only command of conscience. I, too, am a strenuous believer in a Categorical Imperative, but I phrase mine a little more simply. I call it the law that there shall be law. Conscience warns us that acting from mere impulse, non-permanent desire, or reaction from stimulus, has no moral quality. A person is capable of something more than this. His will should express respect for law as law. It is true this is only a part of the story, the philosophic or *a priori* part. Kant calls it the form of ethics. The supplemental matter must be drawn from the special circumstances of the case. Just so, when we are told to love our neighbor, we are not informed whether we should buy him stockings or gloves or indeed whether we should buy him anything. This will vary with the state of the needy one's hands and feet. The precept of love is a Categorical Imperative which applies regardless of circumstances. But these variable conditions are ethically as meaningless when parted from the imperative of love as is love when parted from them. The two belong together. Kant has been foolishly blamed for failing to see the partial character of his Categorical Imperative. But he intended it to be partial. He took upon himself the task of exploring the Metaphysic of Morals and never dreamed of superseding experience in the actual conduct of life. This latter he has treated with much subtlety of observation in a separate paper. But I think he has made it plain that taken by itself conscience is no compendium of diverse instructions as to how we should act in all sorts of cases. I know only one indwelling law, the law that there shall be law. Moral perplexity is possible and not infrequent. We encounter conflicting claims and are obliged to say I would gladly do right if I only could discover what is right. In such cases our only resource is to study the conjunct experience of ourselves and the race and learn what has in the long run proved most favorable for fullness of life. As I have previously remarked, nothing outside life can justify living.

XXIV

Since, in Part I, I have described the great philosophic changes which have come about in my time, it may be interesting to note briefly the political transformations which have attended them. Every age is called a transitional time. And rightly, for change never ceases. But at certain periods changes are so rapid and affect such large tracts of life that they deserve preëminently the name of transitional. It is hardly an exaggeration to say that I shall die in a different world from that in which I was born. At my birth in 1842 there were twenty-two fewer States in our country than at present. We had not begun to acquire foreign possessions, like the Sandwich Islands, Alaska, the Philippines, and islands in the Gulf of Mexico. Two sudden shiftings of population deserve mention, one in Texas in 1848 at the close of the Mexican War, another in 1849 on the discovery of gold in California. The regular connection with the Pacific Coast was by sailing vessel around Cape Horn. The Middle West was thinly settled, Chicago having less than five thousand inhabitants. The first considerable steam railroad, that between Baltimore and Washington, was built in 1844. Of course telegraphs, telephones, electricity, and radio were not in use. For our knowledge of events in Europe we were dependent on foreign correspondents. The first regular steamer, that from Liverpool to Boston, arrived in 1840, taking more than fourteen days for the voyage. As late as 1867, when I crossed, there were only small paddle-wheel steamers, and mine, a Cunarder, took thirteen days.

Few countries in Europe have remained unchanged. Victoria was at my birth in only the fifth year of her long and eventful reign. In France Bourbons were the rulers. In most of my visits to Paris Napoleon III was the Emperor. Two or three revolutions there I have witnessed. Germany was a collection of petty states. In one of them, Württemberg, my University years were spent. Austria was a huge and straggling empire, the overlord of most of Italy. Her quarrels with Hungary drove Kossuth into exile, and I saw him received in Boston in 1852. The Crimean War of 1856, with the later Russo-Turkish wars, profoundly altered the whole East of Europe. Egypt first detached itself from Turkey and then, after the rebellion of Arabi Pasha, came under the control of England. Italy, which throughout my early life had been a collection of states, was united in 1860 by Garibaldi, Cavour, and Victor Emmanuel. France was overrun by Germany in 1870, and then gradually built up the vast French colonies of Algeria and Morocco. Spain went through many transformations, during the nineteenth century losing all her American possessions. The year of my birth saw foreign trade allowed for the first time in half a dozen cities of China. Japan was opened to foreigners in 1854, following the visit of Admiral Perry and the American fleet. India was a private possession of the East India Company till 1858. The Suez Canal was constructed by De Lesseps in 1860; the Panama Canal by the United States in 1914. South Africa was transformed by the Boer War. But it would be tedious to chronicle the changes in the many small countries, particularly those of Africa, Australia, and South America. Since the Great War little remains of what was familiar twenty-five years ago.

XXV

This final section of my paper shall be an anatomy of myself. An autobiographer by his very title announces that he is willing to have strangers draw near and inspect his inward parts. They cannot do so merely by becoming acquainted with the events of his life, for the same events may spring from a wide variety of personal origins. Only the man himself, if self-conscious, frank, and disinterested, can rightly interpret them. This now becomes my interesting and difficult task. I will try to describe the way I am made as I see it.

From childhood I was curious about the significance of that strange creature, a human being, so like, so unlike a machine. Puritanism saved me from any simple solution. It saw depravity and high aspiration living side by side. Fortunately modern study of character has turned in the same direction. Before Boswell, biography was for the most part written either to record occurrences in the life of a king or statesman, or else it had a moral aim and sought through

123

the presentation of some saintly figure to stimulate virtue in others. Boswell for the first time painted a full-length portrait with no other aim than portraiture. Johnson's defects are as manifest as his excellences. In our day Lytton Strachey in England and Gamaliel Bradford in America have taught us that the first step in understanding a character is to note its limitations and see what color they impart to the entire person. President Tucker said to me long ago, 'Don't let your defects bother you. Make yourself strong enough to carry them off.' To the same purport is the warning of Jesus against pulling up tares in a wheat-field. The different roots are too closely intertwined to be lightly torn asunder.

Early I learned that because of an exceptionally bad memory I could never be a great scholar. To no avail were my many attempts at improvement, especially after the reading of themes and examination papers had made the matter every year worse. Encyclopædic learning I must leave to Germans. I regretted still more to find that continuous constructive thinking was forbidden me. Whether I was cut off from this by the general physical weakness of the first half of my life or by special brain conditions, I cannot say. The result was the same; I was not designed for a system-builder.

Now it is foolish to sit lamenting over what one has not. The wisdom of life is to accept whatever comes and extract power from it. Accordingly I turned to criticism. Criticism became my sacred word. Readers of this paper must have been struck with the frequency of its occurrence here. Its simplest definition is the sense of inadequacy. Slightly modified as the Glory of the Imperfect, it appeared as the title of one of my earliest papers. Combined with appreciation of beauty — beauty in poetry, pictures, architecture, or landscape — it becomes a mighty engine, successively revealing what is adequate or harmonious and teasing us to bring this perfection to birth. It has been my guiding principle in many fields. I have altered successfully five houses. I never planned one from the ground up. I need something to begin with and improve. This ethical sense of a better in alliance with its twin sister, the æsthetic, trains practical judgment and makes one a generally useful person, resorted to by many for advice. Such advisory work has brought me much happiness and has enabled me to find situations for a large number of teachers. My recommendations are accepted because they are not generalities, but indicate just the work of which a candidate is capable.

Knowing that I was not a genius, was indeed in most respects less clever than other young men of my years, yet had my own way to make with little assistance, I was early led to feel the importance of work. All I have done has been costly in labor. Nothing in it is spontaneous. I have often thought I was planned for a loafer; but being born in New England was somewhat spoiled in the making. Sometimes I wonder that so many sons of the rich become men of power. They might have lived at ease, and have rotted, if they had not had, a goodly number of them, a sense of moral responsibility to themselves and society. I have needed steady pressure and have had it, thank Heaven.

The greatest longing of my youth was for literary fame. At that time this was a common desire. To-day the desire for wealth has taken its place. But I was badly hampered as a writer. Essentially a solitary, feeble in frame and ill at ease among strangers, I wrote few letters, talked little, and had no promptings to self-expression. Writing has always remained extremely difficult. The blank sheet of paper lying before me waiting to be filled has never ceased to be an object of horror. Yet I have printed seventeen independent volumes and am on the whole glad of the pains they have cost. The lack of fluency has saved me from writing non-sense. Style wins a certain dignity when one feels that the subject has been seen clean through and is meant to be stated just so. Easy writing is usually hard reading. Hard writing, if right methods are employed, makes a reader's work easy. As my modes of writing are the result of a good deal of study, I will sketch some of them here.

The peculiar feature of my writing for publication is the double copy, one for me, one for my reader. Whatever I write to-day is written with the aim of truth and fullness. Into it goes everything which might at this point have a bearing on the argument. But as this draft is merely a gathering of material, it would be hardly intelligible to any one but myself. To-morrow I rewrite this, discharging from my mind all consideration of truth, and studying simply ease of apprehension on the reader's part. The order of the sentences will frequently require revision. Some word or sentence will 'stick out' and attract undue notice. The sentences may have too little variety of pattern. I shall come upon hitches which will oblige a reader to pause an instant. Unnecessary words will be discovered, even repetitions. But everywhere ease should be the one thing sought, the test of its attainment being, Does the page on being read seem short? These two aims, of truth and ease, are apt to be confused by many writers. When they come to their second writing, they are still thinking of accuracy. They remember something which had not occurred to them before, perhaps some qualifying clause which would add a fresh shade of truth, and in it goes, checking the smooth flow of the page and compelling slow reading. This is no time for additions, but for dropping everything that can be spared. Of course some repetition will be useful to save the reader from being forced onward more rapidly than his mind can travel. But it should come in the guise of humor, illustration, or simplification.

One of the commonest hindrances to easy reading is the long sentence. I went through a paper last year which averaged four sentences to a page. It was dismal reading. I had almost forgotten the beginnings of the sentences when I reached their ends. The writer was evidently merely clearing his own mind, with no thought of a reader. Yet I must acknowledge that a long and well-built sentence sometimes adds weight to an argument, while too many short sentences become choppy and annoy the reader with a perpetually fresh start. I am afraid my writing has often this fault. A judicious mixture of longs and shorts is best. The short sentence, too, should have importance, like a headline, unless it is the three or four words which come as a relief at the close of a complicated exposition. In any case the principle is plain: the reader is the important person; devices to engage him will always be in order; the architecture of style must never be forgotten; and ease must be an object of effort.

My procedure in speaking or teaching is different. Most of what I have to say can be found in some book. The only valuable element I can add is myself. Evidently, then, the minute methods I have been prescribing for a writer will be of little use to a speaker. Indeed, if I have a complete draft behind me of what I am going to say, I am wrecked. For the two processes of remembrance and live personal thinking are antagonistic. When I am trying to recall a phrase I cannot think, and while I am thinking words must take care of themselves. Before speaking, I must fill myself freshly with my subject, no matter how familiar it is. I may have spoken on it before, but I must have at hand only so much memoranda as will keep me from sprawling. After some hours of study and reflection, I draw up on a quarter-sheet of paper an outline of the topics I propose to discuss, with special attention to their order. Whatever is simplest and easiest to comprehend should of course come first, whatever is more complicated later. I even assign the amount of time the different portions of my programme will require, but no sentences are written. Then, with a mind stuffed with my subject, an orderly path visible through it, my outline and watch on the table, I stand before my class and begin to think aloud, as for myself, in the plainest language, letting the thought summon its own vocabulary. Somehow or other the personality goes across. It is an untraceable and vitalizing influence, easily catching,

though you can't vaccinate with it. Observe
or try to place it and it disappears. Yet,
while anything already written ruins me, I
find that I speak better on a ground I have
travelled previously. Perhaps while personality demands freedom, it is emboldened by
exercise. Fear is its subtlest foe. Until a
speaker is entirely at ease his hearers will
not be.

But there is more in teaching than this:
there is moral discipline. In it one gets his
best training in Imagination, which once
gained, yes, gained in any considerable degree, invigorates every power of him who
gains it and makes all the world around the
better. For by imagination I mean the
ability to put myself in another's place,
think his thoughts, and state strongly his
convictions even when they are not my own.
Many a worthy man I have known who was
altogether willing to do his share of the
world's work, but was quite shut off from his

fellows by lack of imagination. Men called him selfish, but he was not exactly that, only constitutionally incapable of seeing anything beyond his own horizon. On the other hand, a man of imagination is welcomed everywhere, for he is a better father, friend, minister, lawyer, doctor, author, shopkeeper, or member of society, being able swiftly to perceive the diverse minds of these people and to adapt himself tactfully to each. Why people are willing to face the frictions of life without imagination is a mystery.

A few years of teaching will convince any one of the need, the possibility, and the attraction of acquiring it. Each pupil differs from every other and all stand at a long remove of development from their teacher. To be able to meet them all helpfully has been the fascinating passion of my life. It is a piece of Fine Art in which I have been enabled to meet with some success. Of course I have fallen far short of a perfect

134

teacher. No such being was ever known. But by perpetual criticism I have brought myself to circumvent a new batch of errors almost every year. Before my mind began to fail under my last surgical operation, I think I had attained much of what I sought. To meet every one with considerate tact was becoming almost habitual and the habit bred a dispassionate mind. I do not so often mix desires with my judgments as I see many around me doing.

Professor Shaler once remarked that there were two sets of Professors at Harvard. One was absorbed in private study; another observed also the general course of the University, noted its defects, and was ingenious in proposals for their removal. I have always belonged to this second group. It fits in with my dominant method of criticism — that is, with making my start in a given defect and aiming at betterment. This leaning toward administration has brought me many calls elsewhere. But I have found more interest in the further advancement of what is here. There has been no lack of variety. I have been connected with five Departments — Greek, Philosophy, Divinity, Fine Arts, English — in two of these taking the place of absent Professors. At six of our affiliated Western colleges I was Exchange Professor, and many years before the Great War I was offered the Exchange Professorship in Berlin. This I declined because I was unwilling to meet the Kaiser, whom I regarded as the most dangerous man in Europe. As regards offices, I have been Tutor, Instructor, Curator, Assistant Professor, Professor, Professor Emeritus, Overseer — pretty fully a Harvard man. Harvard and six other universities have given me honorary degrees.

I remember how Dr. Andrew Peabody warned us students one morning at Prayers: 'Young men, be careful what you dream. Dreams are apt to come true.' I dreamed of happy marriage, of a large library, of foreign travel, of clearing my mind of philosophic and religious perplexities, of teaching in some great university, of being widely loved, of strenuous middle life with an old age of health and financial ease, of winning fame, especially as a writer. Looking back I can say I have little more to wish. The years have brought substantially what I asked — opportunity to do useful work as an organizer of one of the most distinguished Departments of our foremost University, with more than fifteen thousand students in my classes and kind faces meeting me wherever I go. Three of my books may live for half a century — my books of affection and gratitude, 'George Herbert,' 'Homer,' and the 'Life of Mrs. Palmer.' The first was not intended for wide circulation, but was an appeal to scholars in behalf of a much misunderstood poet. The London 'Times' gave it two strongly commendatory articles and declared that whoever dealt with Herbert hereafter must take this book into account. The second I tried to restore to nature and redeem from artificial 'Classicism.' The sales of my translation of the Odyssey have increased in each of the thirty-odd years since it was published, during the last three being over forty thousand a year. More than fifty thousand copies of Mrs. Palmer's 'Life' have been sold. She herself has become a kind of patron saint of college girls and has been elected to the Hall of Fame. As I see these things rising behind me they do not seem of my doing. Some greater power than I has been using me as its glad instrument.

THE END

84

...phy of a

		DATE DUE	

54502
1 Aug '4   18 Mar '52   1996
505.90   4744
'6 Oct 4   MAR '56.
3304
5 May '56